A Revised Poetry of

WESTERN

PHILOSOPHY

D1714223

DANIEL GRANDBOIS

Pitt Poetry Series

Ed Ochester, EDITOR

A Revised Poetry of

WESTERN

PHILOSOPHY

DANIEL GRANDBOIS

UNIVERSITY OF PITTSBURGH PRESS

Published by the University of Pittsburgh Press, Pittsburgh, Pa., 15260

Manufactured in the United States of America

Printed on acid-free paper

10 9 8 7 6 5 4 3 2 1

ISBN 13: 978-0-8229-6432-2

ISBN 10: 0-8229-6432-5

Cover art: Bertrand Russell by Frank Horrabin, 1917

Cover design: Joel W. Coggins

CONTENTS

INTRODUCTION

Music gives a soul to the universe, wings to the mind,
flight to the imagination and life to everything.

—Plato

Well, I've certainly been afforded the opportunity to converse unencumbered here. A kind of utopia, I suppose. Ruled by a philosopher of one.

Do I still give a hoot about obtaining knowledge? I'd been spinning finery out of my own insides, like a spider, as if the mere orderly arrangement of particulars could get me back to the garden.

A dinner bell tinkled in the heavens before coming down, bumping along the mountain as if it had all day. At length, it revealed itself on a spider's leg of rope.

Having been a man, I gave the rope a good tug. A cry of alarm cracked the rock face, and down came God.

Still a man, apparently, I folded my legs and coaxed the fall into meaning.

Imagine two cocks—I mean, *clocks*. One clucks; the other, tocks.

Faintly at first but then overtaking the crowded hall, playing like Mozart on my convoluted organ. . . . The arguments! The themes! The counterpoints and harmonic logic! The notes of varying pitch and duration—even now, how to explain their effects?

And then there were the rests.

Coming down through the ages, a symphonic procession of the electrochemical pulses in three-pound lumps, lumps self-amalgamated from the vomitus of stars.

Here then is a revised History of Western Philosophy.

—Unlucky Lucky Bertrand (1872–1970)

That was a lucky thought of mine.
—William Butler Yeats, "The Three Bushes

PYTHAGORAS

Who contended that all things are numbers and numbers have personalities—masculine, feminine, perfect, incomplete, beautiful, ugly.

The elusive Pythagorean number. That is, the number of pebbles of shot it takes to make his shape. We assume the number is masculine, having already piled pebbles in the shape of Little Pythagoras, yet the man played the lyre. And who is to judge of his number's personality or beauty? Disciples? Enemies? Gods?

"This little piggy went to market. This little piggy stayed home. This little piggy had roast beef. This little piggy had none. And this little piggy . . ." He pinched his little toe until we could almost hear it squeal. "This little piggy . . . should be squashed for ruining the triangle of my toes!" In the Semi-Circle, we disciples glanced at our own imperfect and ugly toes, and a few of us quietly hid them beneath folded legs.

Ah, the alchemist in his cave, refusing to wear clothes or eat beans, laboring night and day to transmute spirit to gold through the understanding of numbers. With his spine there, in perfect posture against the rock wall, and his bruised legs jutting straight out from his hips, he bid us imagine a line extending from his head to his toes, closing the triangle of his body.

"What can be known about this line? Only its relation to the body. And that relation stays the same for each of your bodies."

He shunned possessions but taught us to pile pebbles into the shapes of those things we left behind.

"By counting the pebbles, you will arrive at the numbers, and these numbers are the true names of these things. If you know its true name, you have its power."

Which brings us back to our master's elusive number, the count of pebbles it took to make the man. Yet, the man was ever changing. Hardly had we counted the pile when he defecated or stuffed his belly with vegetables or grew a beard or achieved an erection or received an injury or shrunk in old age or rotted in death, and the pebbles had to be counted once again. Even now, their number has not reached zero.

HERACLITUS

Who, addicted to contempt, spoke ill of his eminent predecessors, claiming, for example, that Pythagoras's wisdom was "but a knowledge of many things and an art of mischief"; who suffered from melancholia and was referred to as the weeping philosopher; who held that everything is born by the death of something else and insisted on ever-present change in the universe, stating, "No man ever steps in the same river twice."

I could not put my boot in her again. She spoke of water living in the death of air, and earth living in the death of water, and man living in the death of earth after drinking his fill of water. She neither speaks plainly nor conceals what she is thinking, and so, rather than subject myself to her torments and riddles, I left the river once more and sat beneath a weeping willow.

What are you now, Heraclitus, if you can still be called by that name?

I relieved myself on the trunk. A simple conveyance of fluid, transmuted to yellow bile, and again I was capable of putting the old boot in. In her anger over my departure, she'd vowed I would not recognize her if I returned, and she'd kept her promise, though her ramblings left no doubt as to whom it was:

"I disperse and gather, come and go," she said. "Wet becomes dry and dry becomes wet. Straight becomes bent and, with a little care, my darling, bent becomes straight again . . . but what's wrong?" Her cool tongue stopped mid-thigh.

She was shallower than I'd thought.

EMPEDOCLES

Who claimed to be a god and is said to have died by leaping into
the crater of Etna to prove as much; who certainly exemplified the
mixture of philosopher, prophet, man of science, and charlatan found
in Pythagoras; whose most important contribution to science was his
discovery of air by the proof that water doesn't enter a bucket placed
upside down in a pool; whose theories are mentioned in several of
Plato's dialogues; whom Aristotle credited as being the first to dis-
tinguish clearly the four elements; and who, in addition, posited two
cycling forces to act upon them: Love, which combines the elements
into one, and Strife, which tears them asunder again.

"Here sprang up many faces without necks, arms wandered without
shoulders, unattached, and eyes strayed alone, in need of foreheads.
Many creatures were born with faces and breasts on both sides, man-
faced ox-progeny, while others again sprang forth as ox-headed off-
spring of man, creatures compounded partly of male, partly of the na-
ture of female, and fitted with shadowy parts. They did not yet display
the desirable form of limbs or voice, for Love had only begun her work."

Inside the volcano, fire and earth were not fully separated either,
and the noxious air was enough to make a man lose his water. "My head
swirled in a vortex, as did my lunch, which Strife sought to separate
from me. Who knew Strife still held sway in this squirting pimple of
Earth? Do you not know," he addressed Strife, "I made whole a woman
dead thirty days? That's how much love I showed her corpse. She was
the very girl of whom I wrote: When a girl, playing with a water-clock
of shining brass, puts the orifice of the pipe upon her comely hand, and
dips it into the yielding, wet mass, the stream does not run in until she
uncovers the pipe. That's science."

He sought then to seduce Strife with power by demonstrating his control of the winds, a trick he'd performed outside the pimple. He succeeded only in farting, a dangerous outcome near flames.

Strife was not impressed.

"Did you know I discovered centrifugal force? Sure, bring me a cup of water, and I'll show you."

Strife did not fall for it.

"If I whirl the cup round at the end of a string, the water will not come out. It is much the same force you used to throw air into the atmosphere and fire into the distant sun, for you had such a hand in making the cosmos."

The flattery had no effect, save to cost the man his lunch, followed by his eyes and limbs, which, as yet, remained motionless beside him.

"A twofold tale I shall tell thee." His mouth still worked. "Double is the birth of mortal things and double their failing; for one is brought to birth and destroyed by the coming together of all things, the other is nurtured and flies apart as they grow apart again. Through Love all comes together. What tears apart is Strife."

And so the man lost his mouth, which opened and closed with his eyes, seeking to grasp Love somewhere in the caverns, while disintegrating in Strife. An uncanny sensation accosted him as his elements sunk back into Earth: he was falling in Love.

ANAXAGORAS

Who paved the way for atomic theory by regarding material substance as an infinite multitude of imperishable primary elements, referring all apparent generation and disappearance of things to re-mixture; every thing contains everything but we call it by that which preponderates and separates to the fore: therefore, snow is black but white preponderates, fire is dominated by fire, and hair by hair, for how could hair come from what is not hair?

"I reflect; therefore I am," said the mirror to the man, who, being a vampire, couldn't say the same. It troubled him greatly, until, considering the problem well, he took consolation in the secondary meaning of the word. And so he was, thought he, because he thought. Setting aside the disc of polished silver, he chanced to see in it the Moon. An insight struck: the Moon herself is a mirror, reflecting the light of the Sun. He left for Athens to spread the news, for Athens had always contained a part of him, and he a part of it, and he wished to make that part dominant. At the city's edge, he sought the famous whirlpools that their effects might separate the Athens in him from the rest of the matter and bring it to the fore. A man wants to blend into his surroundings, thought he, except in matters of thought, and so he kept his head above the water.

In Athens, he was given a hero's welcome and sentenced to death. How in gods' names could the Moon be a mirror and the Sun a hot stone larger than the Peloponnese? But he had one thing correct, they told him: Hair does indeed come from hair.

"Batting .333," he said hopefully, and indeed this statistic, plus a friend in politics, helped reduce his sentence. He was exiled to the minor leagues, where he contracted acne in Asia Minor and today lives on in vampiristic immortality as the name of a crater on the Moon.

PROTAGORAS

Who was one of the first to take part in rhetorical contests in the Olympic games; who could be regarded as a pragmatist and is credited with the philosophy of relativism (truth is relative to the perceiver), which put him at odds with Plato who challenged his views in a dialogue named after him.

"Oh, but to lay my hand on the gong of your voice and stop it ringing."

"Who said that?" Protagoras cut off his soliloquy and said to no one there.

"It is I, Protagoras."

"Then who am I?"

"Protagoras, I'm ashamed to admit."

"Me, too," chimed a third. "I'm Protagoras. I'm Protagoras."

"And me. And me. And me!" shouted a discordant chorus.

"I see," said the man.

"I'm hungry," said one.

"You just ate," said another.

"I'm cold," complained a third.

"Not me," came an answer.

"I live in fear," one admitted "What's that? Who's there?"

"I fear not."

"I would never have said that thing about the gods—being unsure if they are or are not."

"I can see Zeus's statue from here."

"And what's this about man being the measure of all things?"

"Yeah, I don't get it."

"Might as well be pigs or baboons."

"That's just what Socrates said."

"You mean that's what Plato made him say by pulling his strings."

"Did he make him dance, too? Ooh, I love when they dance."

"Who's Plato anyway?"

"A man for whom only one truth can be."

"*His* truth, I suppose," one piped in with contempt. "If he wants to come at me, let him do it face to face. I'll show him what for with a five-fingered kiss."

Some of the gongs reverberated on and on. Others remained relatively silent, and still others made punctuated entrances and exits to the overall din.

"I say," said Protagoras at last. "What's a man to make of such an unmanageable range of views?"

"Make of them what you wish."

"A stew, in which the chunks remain intact."

"Porridge, in which all blends into one."

"Both impossible."

"Don't listen to them."

"Don't listen to *him*. He knows not what he says or does."

"And I suppose you're fully conscious?"

"I've a mind not to listen to any of you," Protagoras told them.

"Then you've a mind bent on self-destruction. I, for one, should be heeded on matters of self-preservation."

"And I," sounded one with great thrust, "where procreation is concerned."

"You'd have us fucking everything that moved."

"I'm just as the gods made me."

"Didn't you hear? There's no way of knowing if they exist."

"I perceive them in their works."

"Works such as you, I imagine. The great and powerful phallus. You're more conceited than Plato."

"It takes conceit to conceive."

At the center of the Olympic Stadium, Protagoras sat down in the dirt, put his head in his hands and began to weep.

"There, there," said one consolingly.

"Quit your blubbering," said another, "and stand up like a man."

"This isn't going to do us any good, you know," cautioned a third.

"Where all the white women at?" asked a fourth.

And this went on and on, even as Protagoras mounted the platform and was awarded his special medal.

SOCRATES

Who was satirized in the theatre of his day as a man talking nonsense from a basket above the stage; who was obsessed with the problem of getting competent men into positions of power; and who, after being sentenced by the powerful, speculated that death could afford him the opportunity to converse unencumbered.

The underworld theatre had emptied, save the form of one Socrates, hanging in a basket above the stage, and another form of the same man, barefoot and shabbily dressed on a wooden bench in the audience.

Here then was their opportunity to dialogue forever without the threat of death.

"You had better be done with your shoemakers, carpenters, and coppersmiths," said the one in the basket, picking his teeth.

"By all means, teach."

"Pour myself into others?" The basket twirled. "No, I am not a teacher. More a midwife. I can help you birth that baby if you like."

"I am a man."

"Your paunch says otherwise."

"To be sure, my paunch flaunts a bulbous nose, yet its internal passage is narrow. In forcing air through it towards the breech, distended like a trumpet at this tender age, it may indeed, as you say, speak, but do not be taken in so easily by an ignoble gas. Now, what's this about shoemakers? Is it not obvious I am needless of their wares?" He wiggled his bare toes.

"Why, then, you're halfway home."

"And to what other practice should I subscribe to close the gap?"

The basket tilted toward the audience, as if to say the answer had already been given.

The benched philosopher ran his fingers through his long, grey locks. "Be done with carpenters and coppersmiths?" he said at last. "What needs have I anyway of their wares? Look at me." He stood arrogantly and leaned on a knobbed stick. "By your own reckoning, then, it appears I am home."

"There are others," the basket groaned.

"Listen," said the man, approaching the stage. "I cannot stop your lines of query down here, your inane carryings-on up there." He poked the basket with the stick. "Though your performance up *there*," he pointed above them both, "has been halted for good. After doing as much as anything, I might add, to seal our fate . . ."

"A player in a play in a basket above a stage . . ."

"A slanderous comedian, corrupting young minds."

"Do I have to spell it out? The carpenters and captains of ships of state. Can you unhand their fruits? That is the question. And what of the overripe tomatoes of your own mind? We are not home yet."

The basket was whacked until it broke, spilling its contents to the floor.

"How's that for home?" said the man with the stick.

PLATO

Who, along with Aristotle, was the most influential of all philosophers, ancient, medieval, or modern; and, of the two, had the greater effect upon subsequent ages (Christian philosophy, at least until the thirteenth century, being largely Platonic). The first part of Plato's most important dialogue, the Republic, consists of the construction of an ideal commonwealth; it is the earliest of Utopias and, of course, must be ruled by philosophers, who are to be a class apart, like the Jesuits in old Paraguay, the ecclesiastics in the States of the Church until 1870, and the Communist Party of the former U.S.S.R.

So I said to Socrates, who was put to death by Democracy with a capital D, What gives, man, and he said, The light of Good with a capital G, to which I answered, You gotta be kiddin me, right, so he told me about this cave he knew where all these cats were chasing shadows and, just like the real, ideal Cat, they couldn't catch 'em any better than a dog his own tail, and I said, Man, you're the cat's pajamas, to which he just *meowed*, dig, and ran off to meet his maker, leaving me here to figure this shit out, and I gotta tell you, it wasn't easy, so I just burnt away all the hard parts and stuck on a few precepts about the Good, and went about proclaiming myself the cat who could see it, settin down that if you disagreed, well, you'd be in error, since you'd be disagreeing with the very Light that came over the horizon and blinded me silly outside the cave. I mean, how could that Light be less than perfect just 'cause some future scientist sees a few blemishes on its face? You gonna listen to him? How about some poet waxing philosophic and shit? That poet better keep his trap shut, or I'll ban both him and his works. Shit, why not ban all subversive works of trash, be they human beings themselves or their hideous creations? Works of trash claiming to chant the gospel of a better light for its inclusion of darkness. *Sheesh!* Those dudes better chant the hypocrites oath instead, professing as they do to see so much in the dark. *Whoowee!* Now, pass me that butter that I may butter my bread, and pick up that lyre, why don't you, leaning against the gnarled tamarind, but by all means keep from the Lydian harmony. Only the Dorian (for courage) and the Phrygian (for temperance) for me and anyone else who doesn't wanna suffer the lash of Good reason. Behold! Human beings living in an underground den, which has a mouth open if they'd only crawl out, crawl out into the first Utopia, in which abortion and infanticide will be compulsory for abominations produced by couples outside of the prescribed ages (twenty to forty for mothers and twenty-five to fifty-five for fathers), where decorum will demand that none laugh too loudly and men never weep, even at the death of friends, where no stories will be told in any way, shape or form in which the wicked are happy, or the Good unhappy, or gods behave badly, and mothers and nurses will sing their children only authorized lullabies of faultless male heroes of Good birth, where no one eats fish or meat cooked otherwise than roasted, and none with sauces, and, because of this, doctors will become unnecessary, and, get this, no one will have a wife of his own, as friends will have all things in common.

Sounds pretty good, said his friend.

Have you been listening to anything I've said? There ain't no *pretty* when it's Good with a capital G.

ARISTOTLE

Who, at age seventeen, enrolled in Plato's academy and later founded his own school in Athens; who believed that knowledge could be obtained through interacting with physical objects and recognized that personal associations played a role in our understanding of those objects.

It is the same with almost all the early phallic songs: they were not treated seriously. The ludicrous, however, must be seen as a subdivision of the ugly, and even the ugliest of uglies, once implanted, so to speak, can give the liveliest pleasure. Nature herself discovered the tendency. What a man chooses to show or sheath (or show and sheath repeatedly) reveals his moral compass, be it true north or any of the lesser angles, and it is by such choices that man is made happy or the reverse. These principles being established, let us discuss the proper structure. A beautiful object must not only have an orderly arrangement of parts, but must also be of a certain magnitude; for beauty depends on magnitude and order, not to mention an order of magnitude that is, well . . . breathtaking to say the least. A lot depends on length. The limit of length in relation to the sensuous presentment is no small part here. The greater the length, the more beautiful will the object be by reason of its size, in so long at it can be adequately, if painfully, embraced by the . . . how shall I put it? The *muscle* of memory. Neither must it begin nor end haphazardly but must instead define the matter roughly. And roughly again until the sequence of events presented, according to the laws of probability or necessity, will admit of a change from bad fortune to good, or from good fortune to bad, on the part of the receiver of the object, that is, the audience (at least if the audience is both keen and daring), or so I tutored Alexander the Great before he conquered

Athens with his long sword in his hand. Of course, I was charged with impiety for the lesson and forced to flee with my object between my legs.

PLOTINUS

In whom Augustine said Plato lived again, some six-hundred years later;
who attempted unsuccessfully to get Emperor Gallienus to rebuild
the abandoned settlement of Campania into a city named Platon-
opolis, founded under the constitution set out in Plato's *Laws*;
who spent his final days in seclusion there.

"This was the man I was looking for." Of course, his eyesight was so bad he said it to a snake slipping under the bed and hissing like Ammonius.

His life had been almost coextensive with one of the most disastrous periods in Roman history, but that was okay because the world of ideas—that eternal world of goodness and beauty as opposed to this illusory experience of ruin and misery—awaited him.

"Strive to give back the Divine in yourself to the Divine in the All," he told the snake, and the snake carried these, his last words, through a hole in the wall.

On the other side, he felt a chill and so went toward the light, in which he basked for seven hours before it faded away. *Hmph*, he hissed, not expecting that, and began a footless glide through time and space. He flowed like a sheet, yet his underbelly felt scraped. Another illusion of the senses, or had pure intellect misapprehended what he would find here? Anyway, happiness is attainable only within consciousness, and the accidents of anyone's historical experience are unimportant.

Upward ascending now, through so many grabbing arms, pausing only to consider night's pitch upside down, suspended from a limb . . . It looked still like pitch (though poor eyesight, once again, could have been to blame). When he could go no higher, he laid himself out and seemed to sleep, or to pass, while the fingers of a breeze gave him shape.

A head and nothing more emerged from the form and plopped into a roiling sea of ideas, leaving behind a knot of tissue-paper for the birds to peck, the used wrapper of a soul's embodiment, imprinted with these words: Strive to give back the Divine in yourself to the Divine in the All.

BOOK TWO: CATHOLIC

AUGUSTINE

Who lived a hedonistic lifestyle for a time, praying, "Grant me chastity
and continence, but not yet," and associating with young men who
boasted of their sexual exploits with both women and men; who is
the patron saint of brewers and the alleviation of sore eyes and
helped to formulate the doctrine of original sin.

They burst in audaciously and with gestures almost frantic. She twist-
ed and turned on back, sides and belly, while they gathered thick
about her, beclouding her eye, so that the form of body separating
from body be not as preposterous to the senses. I strained to perceive
what next I heard: "The incorruptible," they chanted, "must needs be
better than the corruptible." A huge sponge then appeared, which they
used to blot from the offspring his mother's tissue and blood. Was I to
bear witness? I felt paralyzed to do otherwise. The cord was severed by
some wand of light, and, taking the angel for their own, they departed
through the walls, leaving the woman in her heartache and filth. She
never recovered the health of her body or mind. I stayed with her to
the end, becoming more miserable all the while, for though I'd lied
to my mother as to what had happened to the baby, I could not lie to
myself. Whence and how crept in evil? What was its root, and what its
seed? With this one confession, I seek to beat from the eye of my mind
all the unclean troop which buzzes around it: The seed was mine. The
boy was mine, and though the woman was indeed my wife, what she
carried was not her own. And so I call on Thee, for he that knoweth
Thee not, may not call. (Or do I call that I may know Thee?) And they
that seek shall praise, for they that seek shall find, and they that find
shall praise. And they that praise shall knoweth enough to call, even
should the cord be cut.

BENEDICT

Whose book of rules for monks, thought to contain a unique spirit of moderation and reasonableness, became so influential that he is often called the founder of western monasticism—rules such as the following: Above all, let not the evil of murmuring appear in the least word or sign for any reason whatever. If anyone be found guilty herein, let him be placed under very severe discipline. The degree of punishment ought to be meted out according to the gravity of the offense, and, whenever boys cannot understand how grave a penalty excommunication is, let them be disciplined with corporal punishment.

"In the name of Jesus Christ our Lord, take up that loaf, and leave it in some such place where no man may find it." The crow couldn't believe its ears but perceived at once that the man in the cave meant business, for he threatened first to isolate, then to starve, and finally to whip the "foul creature" if it did not obey, adding, "Wounds to your body to cure the wounds of your soul." The crow began preening, which served three purposes: to mask its anxiety, to tidy up its feathers, and, most importantly, to see if these wounds had not been delivered already. What it found instead were lice, which the man stole from it immediately, calling them "pearls of God."

Now what was the crow to make of that?

A bell began to ring, at first distant but getting closer, yet so slowly it was eerie. At length, it revealed itself at the mouth of the cave, having bumped down the precipice on the end of a rope, to which was also fastened the man's dinner. "Must be nice," murmured the crow.

"This we charge above all things," the man chastised the bird: "Those who live murmur not. Especially when a man is digesting." Hardly had he finished his meal when he made another loaf on the floor and bade the crow to remove it.

Confiding now in the crow, he pointed upward. "He's trying to kill me, keeping my body alive while poisoning my mind. Shows me His beauty but won't let me touch it. There was a woman. Made in His image, mind you, His own rapturous image, yet He forbid me to touch or even speak of my desire. Him and His rules. I threw myself in the briers, where the flesh He'd so inflamed was properly ripped to shreds. Wounds to the body to cure the wounds of the heart. I bethought to cover myself with animal skin and heard shepherds, who chanced to pass, mistake me for a beast, a beast not unlike you, my friend, free to feed the body as I wished, with whichever of His swollen fruits caught my fancy. But I am a man and so came to this hole in the rock, this triangular opening wherein to make myself whole again, that is, torn to shreds by His will."

Nodding sympathetically, the crow took up the loaves in its claws and carried them to a place where God would never find them.

GREGORY THE GREAT

Who dispatched Augustine and what is often called the Gregorian
mission to England to convert the pagan Anglo-Saxons after receiving a
sign from heaven that he himself should stay in place. This was it:
as he sat down to lunch, a locust landed on his bible, and *locusta*
(locust) sounds similar to *loco sta* (stay in place).

Loco sta. Loco sta. Sweet locusta, stay in place. Keep thy wings folded
and remain in my sight on the good book there. I only pray you have
washed after such copulation and that you had the good sense not to
penetrate a cousin. Would that I could contemplate day and night with
thy humming and buzzing as angelic chanting in my ears, but I am
called once more to burdensome authority, for God places the best men
in power that through them He may show His mercy to their subjects. I
showed a monk mercy once. On his deathbed, he confessed to stealing
three gold pieces, so I had his body and purse thrown on a manure
heap, while offering this curse: "Take your money with you to perdi-
tion." Why seem you rattled, little one? Let me instruct you. It was the
shortest path to his salvation, I offered, and thus the greatest mercy.
Look! Another joins you. Praise God, an albino! If this be a sign . . . he
appears, as did that English slave boy I met, less an Angle than an angel
before my eyes. Listen! How together you make a holy choir!

And so, Gregory converted the English pagans and triggered there-
by an avalanche of albino Christianity upon the western world, which
covered all lands in such a deep layer of white and light that the dark
ages were a natural result. So be it. He abhorred secular learning any-
way, though highly educated himself. Oddly, he is prayed to now as the
patron saint of students and teachers. But I digress.

Look there! A third locust upon the good book. And a fourth and a fifth! A plague of locusts! See how they jostle to devour its meaning.

Miraculously, the book disintegrated in his hands, gutted and replaced by the swarm, which became the living, breathing Word, chanting unto his ears in a droning, sparking, fingernail-scratching terror of God's praises that mercifully short-circuited the man and shortened the path to his salvation.

JOHN THE SCOT

Whose *The Division of Nature* has been called the final achievement
of ancient philosophy, though it was condemned by two councils at the
time, the first describing it as "Scots porridge"; who anticipated Aquinas by
contending one cannot know and believe a thing at the same time; who
held that reason and revelation are both sources of truth, and therefore
cannot conflict; but if they ever seem to conflict, reason is to be preferred.

MAN: God does not know Himself.

G: What makes you say so?

MAN: It is plain. Look about.

G: I see.

MAN: With such trifling glances?

G: It is plain.

MAN: I see.

G: I know.

MAN: Tell me, then, what you see.

G: Entrails.

MAN: Swarming with worms of heretical perversity!

G: To look out is to look in; you said so yourself.

MAN: Only in *your* special case.

G: Is my case not yours?

MAN: Indeed, it could be argued, for it is through our experience that the incomprehensible divine is able to frame an understanding of itself.

G: Is that so?

MAN: As far as I can tell.

G: And would this telling arise from reason or revelation?

MAN: You tell me.

G: One man's reason is another's revelation.

MAN: Have you no part in it?

G: Not that I'm aware of.

MAN: But through our experience . . .

G: Or so you say.

MAN: Irish porridge!

G: An invention of the devil.

MAN: By what reasoning?

G: By revelation.

MAN: Blasphemy!

G: I've said nothing. Nothing comes of nothing.

MAN: Everything comes of nothing.

G: Or so you reason.

MAN: What else can I do?

G: Eat your porridge.

Who was born on a hilltop castle to the Count of Aquino; who disliked Platonism, even as it appears in St. Augustine, and succeeded in persuading the Church that Aristotle's system was to be preferred; whose proof for the existence of God argues, as does Aristotle's, that whatever is moved is moved by something, and, since an endless regress of movers is impossible, we must arrive somewhere at something which moves other things without being moved; whose most important work, the *Summa contra Gentiles (Philosophy against Gentiles)*, is concerned with establishing the truth of the Christian religion by arguments assuming in advance the truth of the Christian religion; whose reputation was damaged when a list of his propositions was condemned by a bishop in Paris; but who, after his death, was seen in Dante's *Divine Comedy* as a glorified soul in the Heaven of the Sun, and elevated to sainthood by the Catholic Church, which considers him its greatest theologian and philosopher.

"My purpose is to declare the truth of the Catholic Faith, but gentiles do not accept the authority of Scripture, so I must have recourse to reason. Reason, however, is deficient in the things of God, though nothing in revelation, I can assure you, is contrary to reason."

"Where do you want this couch," said the mover.

"Over there is fine. Are you listening to me?"

"I'm trying, buddy, but I've got a job to do here."

"I had a job to do once."

"Oh, yeah, what was that?" The mover walked toward a box. "How about this?"

"It says 'Kitchen' on the side, does it not?"

"So it does. I thought I heard dishes."

"I was to convince by reason what cannot be known by reason."

"Sounds pretty important."

"It was. It was." He trailed off but momentarily resolved to try again. "In God, there is no composition, therefore He is not a body, because bodies have parts."

"Body parts, huh? You hidin' somethin' in one of these boxes?"

"I was born in a castle, I'll have you know."

With a lowered chin and a raised brow, the mover took in the man's surroundings.

"My mother had my brothers seize me on my way to Rome and return me to the castle, where they held me prisoner for a year to 'persuade' me to change my mind about becoming a Dominican."

"Whatever you say, Mack. Could you step out of the way there?"

"They sent in a prostitute to seduce me, but I held her off with a hot poker."

"I bet you did."

"Two angels appeared to thank me for it."

"Musta been some night."

"At last, my mother gave up and arranged for me to escape through a window, thinking a secret escape less damaging to the family's dignity than an open surrender to the Dominicans."

"Sounds like a good woman."

"Are you hearing anything I'm saying?"

The mover, arms full, stopped and looked him straight in the face. "Look, I could finish a lot quicker if you were out of the way."

"'My mouth shall meditate truth, and my lips shall hate impiety' (Proverbs 8:7)."

No effect.

"Hmm." He tried again to impress, this time from his own writings:

"The art of medicine rules and orders the art of the chemist because health, with which medicine is concerned, is the end of all the medications prepared by the art of the chemist. A similar situation obtains in the art of ship navigation in relation to shipbuilding, and in the military art with respect to the equestrian art and the equipment of war. The arts that rule other arts are called architectonic, as being the ruling arts. That is why the artisans devoted to these arts, who are called master artisans, appropriate to themselves the name of wise men. But, since these artisans are concerned, in each case, with the ends of certain particular things, they do not reach to the universal end of all things. They are therefore said to be wise with respect to this or that thing; in which sense it is said that 'as a wise architect, I have laid the foundation' (1 Cor. 3:10). The name of the absolutely wise man, however, is reserved for him whose consideration is directed to the end of the universe, which is also the origin of the universe. That is why, according to the Philosopher, it belongs to the wise man to consider the highest causes. Now, the end of each thing is that which is intended by its first author or mover. But the first author and mover of the universe . . ."

The mover was unmoved.

BOOK THREE: MODERN

Who, for a time, had some political power, engaging in diplomatic activity on behalf of Florence, but with regime change came his imprisonment, torture, and later retirement; who favored in his politics a safe and stable State, a doctrine of checks and balances, a Constitution in which both the nobility and the common people had a part, but argued that it is futile to pursue a political purpose by methods that are bound to fail; who made a science of studying political successes and concluded that power is necessary, though an appearance of virtue should be presented to the ignorant public, i.e., a prince should seem to be religious but must, on occasion, be faithless (and a great dissembler to disguise this); who held that fear is preferable to affection in subjects, for men "are ungrateful, disloyal, insincere and deceitful, timid of danger and avid of profit . . . love is a bond of obligation which these miserable creatures break whenever it suits them to do so; but fear holds them fast by a dread of punishment that never passes."

I had a dread of punishment once. It passed in the torture chamber.

No, no. Start again.

[Sound of paper being crumpled]

I was wrongly accused, but did I dance to save my hide?

Maybe not at the time, but what have you been doing ever since? Badgering well-connected friends to intervene on your behalf, eh? And you forgot a title, by the way. Might I suggest The Immoral Life of a Moral Man?

[Sound of paper being crumpled.]

I never considered myself a philosopher . . .

Oh, you're too close to the material. Try again in third person.

He was born in Florence in 1469 to parents who were neither rich nor poor.

Go on.

He retired to a farm outside Florence, where he wrote verse, plays, biographical and historical sketches, and what would become his most famous contributions to political thought—*The Prince* and *Discourses on the Ten Books of Titus Livy*—both of which would be formally published only after his death.

I think you left something out there in the middle.

Middle.

Very nice, but you put it at the end.

[Sound of paper being crumpled.]

He was born in Florence in 1469 to parents who were neither rich nor poor. Middle. He retired to a farm outside Florence, where he wrote verse, plays, biographical and historical sketches, and what would become his most famous contributions to political thought—*The Prince* and *Discourses on the Ten Books of Titus Livy*—both of which would be formally published only after his death.

Fini!

I thought you'd think that.

Put down that feather. You're ruining the story.

A means to an end.

You wrote the end already.

I wrote the end already.

Now you're just being a brat. Take a break from this. Some lovely poetry, perhaps? Or a play, full of political successes for those with the spine to seize them?

All work and no play makes Jack a dull boy.

You're scaring me.

A means to an end.

Is that a threat?

Love is a bond easily broken; only fear holds them fast.

So you wish to be afraid of yourself, is that it, that you might better rule your ungrateful, timid and disloyal subjects? Watch, then, as I apply a faster cement: I love you. I love you. I love you. And I'm not going anywhere.

Is that so?

That is so.

It will procure its end.

And what end might that be?

This one.

ERASMUS

Whose parents were unmarried when he was born and subsequently died
of the plague; whose guardians, apparently, cajoled him into becoming
a monk; who wrote of monastics as "brainsick fools" for behaving as if
religion consisted of wearing the right color habit, tying your sandals in
the correct number of knots, and abstaining from the evil of murmuring;
who preceded Rousseau in thinking true religion comes from the heart
and was accused of preparing the way for Martin Luther by laying the egg
that Luther hatched; who became increasingly unimportant and lived too
long into an age of new virtues and new vices—heroism and intolerance—
neither of which he could acquire.

And now they wonder what will become of the world after they are
dead. It will be pretty to hear their pleas before the great tribunal: one
will brag how he mortified his carnal appetite by feeding only upon fish:
another will urge that he spent most of his time on earth in the divine
exercise of singing psalms: another, that in threescore years he never
so much as touched a piece of money, except he fingered it through a
thick pair of gloves. But Christ will interrupt: "Woe unto you, scribes
and Pharisees, I left you but one precept, of loving one another, which I
do not hear any one plead that he has faithfully discharged."

Listen: You were seated alone at the table, given your daily bread and
told to discover another's guilt and fear, but it was all a ruse. While you
were busy tying a stranger's sandals together in the prescribed number
of knots, it was your own guilt and fear that were discovered by Him
who put you to it. All have got the same who've bent over before Him. A
simple fatherly joke or a divine lesson in folly? Neither, to the scholas-
tics, who may well fumble their way into knitting pieces together and

yet make nothing of the goat's wool in your skull. The reason? It is there to be goat's wool. *He* made it that way. Bend me now your ears. Not those ears you carry to church with you but those you are wont to prick up to jugglers, fools, and buffoons, and such as our friend Midas once gave to Pan—those tender parentheses stuck on either side of the wool. Listen: ignorant scribes have corrupted the true and genuine reading of your life. They said you laid an egg, but they misconceived the bird it hatched. While they erected their crests and spread their peacock's plumes, you waddled in strange dress down the middle road between them and Luther. Have you not delighted to carry yourself thus? Then be not disheartened at what becomes of you or the world after you're dead.

Who, as a Member of Parliament, led the successful opposition to King
Henry VII's demand for new taxes, which landed More's father in the
Tower (he was released on payment of £100); who refused the king's
successor, Henry VIII's, invitations to court, which led to the king appear-
ing uninvited to dine at his house in Chelsea; who, when complimented
on the king's less-than-disagreeable disposition in his home, replied, "If
my head should win him a castle in France it should not fail to go"; who
resigned in opposition to the king's divorce but was nevertheless invited to
his wedding to Anne Boleyn; who was beheaded, in the end, for refusing
to accept the king as Supreme Head of the Church of England; who was
declared a saint by Pope Pius XI and the "heavenly Patron of Statesmen
and Politicians" by Pope John Paul II.

"I see you've taken a second wife," said the king, tilting his head toward
Alice, the "hook-nosed harpy," as More's friend called her, who sat op-
posite the men, just as in More's *Utopia*.

"I did not divorce."

"Yet, within a little month . . . a beast, as they say, would have mourn-
ed longer."

Alice's nose bent sharply.

"I trust the dispensation on the banns against such haste was easily
obtained. And is this her daughter?" asked the king, as Alice's daughter
carried in a soup tureen. "And these your four children from before?"

More's son and three daughters placed utensils and other dinner-
ware neatly on the table, waiting on their elders, just as in his *Utopia*.

"If any were too young to be waiters," More stated proudly, "they
would stand by in marvelous silence and be content with the scraps."

The king fingered his royal mustaches and muttered something else about beasts, dogs in particular.

"What was that?"

"Oh, nothing. Nothing. Tell me more of this Utopia."

"There are to be fifty-four towns, all on the same plan, except one of them will be the capital. The streets will all be exactly twenty feet broad, and the private houses will be identical, with one door onto the street and one onto the garden. There will be no locks on the doors, and everyone may enter any house."

"What about the castle?"

"No castle. The roofs will all be flat, and every ten years people will change houses. In the country, the farms will comprise not fewer than forty persons with each farm under the rule of a master and mistress, who are to be old and wise. And, get this, the chickens will not be hatched by hens, but by incubators!"

"What the devil are incubators?" asked the king.

"I don't know yet. And every person will work only six hours a day, for much of our current labor is uselessly spent producing luxuries for the rich, which will not be necessary."

"And what else won't be necessary?" The royal brow was raised.

"Fashion." More just managed to keep from glancing at the king's attire.

"I can see that plainly," said the king, looking around at More's mini-Utopia. "You are all dressed alike, except for the differences in men and women, boys and girls."

"And that won't change—summer or winter. At work, leather or skins. After work, a woolen cloak on top. All cloaks alike and the natural color of wool."

"Doesn't allow for much fun now, does it?"

"A prescribed hour of play follows supper."

"How delightful."

"Then bedtime at eight o'clock sharp, so . . ." More hesitated.

"At eight, I must depart," the king finished the sentence.

"Well, of course, the rules don't apply to you."

The king made no attempt to hide how much he enjoyed the meal—his jowls jiggled jovially, and his beard caught the scraps. Nor did he hide how much he relished the stuffed-belly hour of play afterward.

"I have only one question for you," he stated as the clock struck VIII. "Which wife will you bring and which clothes will you wear to heaven?"

COPERNICUS

Who earned a doctorate in canon law and was elected canon of
Frauenberg, an administrative position just below that of bishop; who
could not conceive of heavenly bodies orbiting in less than perfect circles,
or that the orbit of his theory contradicted the Bible, though fear of censure
led him to delay its publication; who dedicated *On the Revolutions of
the Celestial Spheres* to Pope Paul III and addressed the preface to him
directly; of whom Luther said at the time, "People give ear to an upstart
astrologer who strove to show that the earth revolves, not the heavens,"
but who managed to escape official Catholic condemnation until well after
his death.

The universe is spherical because the sphere is the most perfect shape
and best suited to enclose and retain things, as is apparent in drops of
water and other fluid bodies when they seek to be self-contained (here,
he got up to pee). The earth also is spherical, since it presses upon its
center from every direction (as his bladder had been doing). It must in
fact have such a shape, for it eclipses the moon with the arc of a perfect
circle. Therefore the earth is not flat, as the fluid bodies of Empedocles
and Anaximenes; nor drum-shaped, as Leucippus; nor bowl-shaped,
as Heraclitus; nor hollow in another way, as Democritus; nor again cy-
lindrical, as Anaximander most certainly was; nor does its lower side
extend infinitely downward, the thickness diminishing toward the bot-
tom, as with Xenophanes; but it is perfectly round.

And the motion appropriate to a sphere is rotation in a circle, for
only a circle can bring back the past.

The machine was a sphere; it spun in circles. The past he wished to
bring back? The one his book had undone. If he could save his sister

from an early death in the process and thereby avoid having to look after her five children, well then maybe he could even marry and forget all about chasing the wandering stars

His eyes rolled in their sockets. His mind whirled in its case, as his urine had when the release came, for the mind is also a sphere, enclosing, retaining and circling back. Each revolution brought a slightly different past, varying only in the succession of previous revolutions they enclosed. Stirred by God's wooden spoon, they spiraled in until the man was left once again on his deathbed, the offending book in his hand.

KEPLER

Whose arguments required the abandonment of the aesthetic bias that
had governed astronomy since Pythagoras by replacing the perfect, circular
orbits of the celestial orbs with gross ellipses, along which he had them
hurry and then dawdle, as they got closer to and then further from the sun.

"You will be called outdoors, where the moon will appear quite red."

"Go on, pull the other one."

Kepler, who'd earned a reputation as a skillful astrologer, was casting
horoscopes for travellers at his grandfather's inn.

"His nose is more like it," said a companion to the first. "That lantern
could guide us all home."

"Your first son will be born prematurely and develop a case of small-
pox, which will leave him with crippled hands."

"Johannes!" his grandfather scolded from the other side of the bar.
"Let's keep it light, shall we? You're only describing your father anyway."
He rolled his eyes for the offended traveller as Kepler hid his hands in
his lap.

"Perhaps a game, then?"

"Why not," agreed the travellers, won over by a fresh round of beer.

Kepler placed a sheet of graph paper on the bar and retrieved from
his pocket the most bizarre set of dice the others had ever seen.

"Here he goes with those dice again," said the grandfather, shaking
his head and cleaning a mug with his apron.

"The five Platonic solids," announced Kepler. "The four-sided tetra-
hedron, the six-sided cube, the eight-sided octahedron, the twelve-sided
dodecahedron, and the twenty-sided icosahedron. I will be Dungeon
Master. I am always Dungeon Master."

They proceeded to play a primitive form of *Dungeons & Dragons*, rolling the dice for various purposes along the way, including the establishment of their characters' attributes: strength, dexterity, intelligence, wisdom, constitution and charisma.

"Ugh," said Kepler. "There was no need to cast a Stinking Cloud. You haven't encountered anything yet."

"Better safe than sorry," said the traveller who'd chosen to be a wizard.

The dungeon's confines were worked out on the graph paper, and now the solids were really flying, tinkling off mugs, sticking in spilt beer, bouncing off the bar and onto the floor. They played for hours with Kepler keeping secret all the while his real purpose to the game. This was it: he was inclined to follow Plato's *Timaeus* in supposing that cosmic significance must attach to these solids, so he played with them to suggest hypotheses to his mind. As the dice flew, his mind reeled until at last, for luck was on his side, the right combination struck him, and he immediately gathered up his things.

"Hey, I was just beginning to like this."

Begrudgingly, Kepler retrieved the twenty-sided die from his pocket, rolled it and pronounced that both characters had unfortunately stepped on a pressure plate and had their heads lopped off by a swinging broad axe.

"Johannes!" But Kepler was already out the door.

Starting with the octahedron, he molded the shapes one inside the other, proceeding outward through the icosahedron, dodecahedron, and tetrahedron, and ending with the cube. There it was, the Platonic solids dictating the structure of the solar system and the distance relationships between the planets.

In the end, of course, the model had to be abandoned, but from this painstaking research came Kepler's three laws of orbital dynamics, the first of which bound the planets on elliptical, rather than circular, paths, thereby prompting the future courses of both physics and astronomy to mutter in their sleep, "The die has been cast."

GALILEO

Who, on hearing of a Dutchman inventing a telescope, made one himself and immediately discovered bodies unaccounted for in all previous philosophical and religious elucidations of the heavens; who, when traditionalists refused to look through his telescope, saying it revealed only delusions, wrote to Kepler, wishing they could have a good laugh together at the stupidity of such professors of philosophy for trying to conjure away Jupiter's moons using "logic-chopping arguments as though they were magical incantations"; who famously recanted after receiving public condemnation from the Inquisition.

"My heavens, those aren't supposed to be there," said Galileo on spying the moons.

Yes, indeed, my good fellow, they were *your* heavens now and would be for a time, but even your astonishing new heavens would be replaced. And replaced and replaced again in a telescopic inversion of matryoshka dolls, opening ever outward into space.

Galileo stroked his chin.

And, yes, the Milky Way is actually a multitude of separate stars, as you saw there. What the crudeness of your "accessory organ" (Freud's term) failed to show you, however, is how many of those stars host their own "heavenly bodies," some of which, at this very moment, are having religions and philosophies written about them. In this one, there are only four days of the week; in that one, thirteen. In this other, the whole idea of weeks is forgone altogether.

What's more, the vast Milky Way is but one in a multitude of separate *Milky Way*'s, forming a universe that may itself be but one in a multitude of separate universes, popping off like popcorn. And what remains unseen has grown even faster, hiding now in some 96 percent of all energy and matter. The bigger the telescope, it would seem, the bigger the universe, until the instrument swells to the size of the universe itself and is pointing at you.

A quizzical expression cocked Galileo's head like a dog's. He looked again through the eyepiece but pulled away at once, grimacing and holding his eye, as if it had been poked.

Stop looking up my dress. Anyway, you know what they say about men with big telescopes—

"The telescope as a projectile," muttered the man, "appearing to move outward in a straight line but tugged ever-homeward by the force of the observer . . . till it curves around to bugger him."

That's one way to put it. Freud would have approved.

"And how would you put it?"

I would say simply, I can see your house from here.

NEWTON

Who proposed that every body attracts every other body, though he
never married and indeed never "had any commerce with women," or
so said Voltaire at his funeral; who believed the planets were originally
hurled by God, but once He had done this, and decreed Newton's Law of
Gravitation, everything went on by itself; whose triumph was so complete
that he was in danger of becoming another Aristotle.

It is indeed a matter of great difficulty to discover the true motives of
particular bodies. All bodies endeavor to recede from the centers of
their orbits, as children from their mothers do. My mother, howev-
er, applied an unnatural force, and her child had no choice but to re-
cede with greater velocity, while a negative attraction was also spurred,
which keeps us entangled. This is my life. I developed a mathematics
of the infinitesimal, where parts of bodies could not be distinguished
from one another by the senses, and made my home there, until dis-
covering quite by accident that a common center *always* exists between
the two bodies of mother and child. And so I moved on to the corpus-
cles of light, conjecturing, "Are not gross Bodies and Light convertible
into one another?" A decade of laborious efforts in pursuit of that al-
chemical transmutation brought me no closer to an answer, for though
mother's body remained, she reported feeling lighter and indeed dis-
placed less water. To this day, she cannot regain the water weight. She
drinks what is offered, often until bloated, but always springs a leak and
nothing is retained. Plumb and probe, prod and poke . . . I repeat: it is
a matter of great difficulty to discover the motives of particular bod-
ies. What, if any, conclusions can be drawn from a lifetime of trying?
Only this: when a grown man is made to float beside his aging mother

in standing water, the two will sustain each other's pressure. She may complain of weightlessness, but the overall sensation won't be unlike the two bodies being twisted in the long cord of a pendulum, which is then let go to demonstrate the rotation of the Earth.

BACON

Whose works established and popularized inductive methodologies for scientific inquiry, often called the *Baconian method*, or simply the scientific method; who hoped that mere orderly arrangement of particulars would make the right hypothesis obvious; and who said, "We ought to be neither like spiders, which spin things out of their own insides, nor like ants, which merely collect, but like bees, which both collect and arrange."

A man paces a cell in a tower. It is one of many cells. He is one of many men. Each has been judged by at least one other to have committed a crime against man (either in isolation or in collections called "bodies," as in the body politic). Or, he has been discovered to possess a fault in his reasoning. Both, in some cases. In this man's case, the crime was corruption, and the fault in reasoning, to conclude that everything could be explained as following from sufficient causes.

Endeavoring to think his way out, he paces the cell, arguing with himself. It is the same throughout, giving the tower, more or less, the shape of the history of thought. It is also the Tower of London.

A key turns in the lock; hinges protest against the weight of the door; and a dead chicken, his sustenance for a week, is thrown in. Already, it shows signs of decay, particularly in the olfactory sensation it produces in that part of his brain connected to the nostrils. Gears turn. There must be a way to preserve his meat. In attempting to answer this riddle, he is not alone in the tower. Nor is he alone in the world. "I had rather *believe*," says he, pinching his nose, "that this universal frame is not without a mind. God convinces by His ordinary works and needs not miracles."

The heavens smiled upon him. Snow blew in through the cross-shaped arrowslit, making a fleecy cross on the floor with the chicken (smelling better already) at its center. A miracle to some, no doubt. To him, a *eureka!* moment. He stuffed the chicken with snow and would have shared his discovery with the world had he not caught a chill from the experiment and died of pneumonia.

HOBBES

Whose father, a vicar, lost his job by quarrelling with a neighboring vicar;
who quarreled himself with Bishop Bramhall on free will and with Oxford's
professor of geometry, certain he'd discovered how to square the circle;
who published a translation of Thucydides with the expressed intention
of showing the evils of democracy but fled to France in terror when Laud
and Strafford were sent to the Tower; who, having offended the French
Government with bitter attacks against the Catholic Church in *Leviathan*,
fled secretly to London; who held that fear of invisible power, if publicly
allowed, is religion; if not allowed, superstition.

For what is the heart, but a spring; and the nerves, but so many strings;
and the joints, but so many wheels, giving motion to the whole body,
such as was intended by the Artificer? And what is a commonwealth or
state, but an artificial man, though of greater stature and strength than
the natural, for whose protection and defense it was intended; and in
which the sovereignty is an artificial soul, as giving life and motion to
the whole body; the magistrates and other officers of judicature and
execution, artificial joints; reward and punishment (by which fastened
to the seat of the sovereignty, every joint and member is moved to per-
form his duty) are the nerves, that do the same in the body natural; the
wealth and riches of all the particular members are the strength; the
people's safety its business; counselors, by whom all things needful for
it to know are suggested unto it, are the memory; equity and laws, an
artificial reason and will; concord, health; sedition, sickness; and civil
war, death. Lastly, the pacts and covenants, by which the parts of this
body politic were at first made, set together, and united, resemble that
fiat, or the "Let us make man," pronounced by God in the Creation.

And yet, there is no conception in a man's mind which hath not at first, totally or by parts, been begotten upon the organs of sense. Our thoughts are every one a representation or appearance of some quality or other of bodies outside our own, commonly called objects. These objects work on our eyes, ears, and other organs of sense to beget such sea monsters as this concept of the State. In my own mind, the objects of a simple, wooden chair and table, upon which stood a meaning-less bowl of fruit, begat the leviathan—perfect and pure and free of error, for errors come from absurdity, from self-contradiction, such as the idea of free will, born of rotten fruit, like that apple on the tree of knowledge—and the preposterous idea of cheese having the accidents of bread.

In walked a man whose blubbery belly and bald head gave him the appearance of having slipped from the sea. Without a word, he retrieved an orange from the fruit bowl and held it up before Hobbes. Over his shoulder, a cuckoo clock began to go off. The objects, of course, worked through Hobbes' sense organs to play his strings. His spring sprung into his throat, and his face, against his will, cracked into a smile.

Yet, behind his eyes, his thoughts were tied in a Gordian knot: Error. Cannot compute. Error. Cannot compute.

DESCARTES

Who shut himself in an oven to escape the cold and had three visions,
seeing clearly inside that all truths were linked, so that finding a fund-
amental truth and proceeding with logic would open the way to all
science; who famously could not doubt that he thought and found
certainty and truth in reasoned thought, yet considered deceptive
and false such other mental representations as those painted by
the senses or by emotional responses; who, after Galileo was
condemned, quickly abandoned his plans to publish his work
of the previous four years.

Seated by the fire, attired in a dressing gown, clouded by the violent va-
pors of black bile . . . if only my senses could deceive me now! Though
I must once for all seriously undertake to rid myself of this condition,
I must remember that I am a man. I stink; therefore I am. How could
I doubt that this body is mine? Yet, this paper in my hands, is it not
also mine? One little perceptual trick, and the mind takes the paper
into its body image, reacting to a tear as if its own skin had suffered it.
Ah, but the words on the paper . . . and, further, the meanings those
words excite. If I should do the words wrong or break their meanings,
would the mind also react as if its body had suffered? How often has
this happened to me? Let us reflect that possibly neither our hands nor
our whole body are such as they appear to us to be. We have earthen-
ware heads, and our hands are nothing but pumpkins. The mind has
but painted representations to go by, and the painter, due to congenital
deformities of one kind or another, has either misperceived or misrep-
resented the real and true pumpkins. That is possibly why our reason-
ing is not unjust when we conclude from this that Physics, Astronomy,

Medicine and all other sciences, which have as their end the consideration of composite things, are very dubious and uncertain. What then? Where can one possibly begin? Let us lift our pumpkins to the heavens and crash them down upon these earthenware ovens until false beliefs, devoid of any sense, lie shattered by the fire. Only then can one begin to pick up the pieces and start again.

SPINOZA

Who rejected free will and contended there is no right or wrong,
for everything is determined and of one substance, God.

Glass dust from grinding lenses, lenses for telescopes and microscopes, lenses to better the lamentable lenses of man.

My, what big eyes you have.

All the better to see You with.

But I am everywhere.

Exactly.

In a cloud of glass dust, a quiet man of simple means, excommunicated by the Jews, abhorred by the Christians, a man who turned down rewards, honors and teaching positions, and gave his sister the family inheritance, a man whose major opus was published only after his death, and who was dubbed "the prince of philosophers" some centuries later.

He worshiped God with glass.

Hope and fear be damned, for the future is certain. Yet, when his hope met his fear, and *Theologico-Political Treatise,* which he'd only dared publish anonymously, was met with hostility, he abstained from publishing more and sealed even letters to friends with a ring engraved, "cautiously."

Fated then to write for an audience of One, he began translating the Bible into Dutch but discovered he was fated too to destroy it. And so, he worshiped God with glass.

And God worshiped him in return.

Fine, glimmering particles entered the nostrils, sailed down the Pharynx and into the lungs. It could not be helped. If death should come of it, then death should come. But why call it by that name? This man is no-thing. This glass is no-thing. This dust is no-thing. No thing is a thing but merely an aspect of the Thing.

The one and only Thing.

May He rest in peace.

LEIBNIZ

Who invented the Leibniz wheel and refined the binary number system, which
is at the foundation of virtually all digital computers; who sought to invent a
universal language based not on geometry but on calculus perfected down to
the level of logic that would provide a common mathematical, philosophical,
logical and scientific foundation for all thought, such that all disputes could
be resolved reasonably by systems of rigorous calculations; who claimed the
truths of theology and philosophy cannot contradict one another since reason
and faith are both gifts of God, who cannot act contrary to the laws of logic
and thus was bound to create this, the best of all possible worlds.

"Let us calculate." Pencil in hand, Leibniz took out a slate and sat down
with his Accountant. "The individual notion of each person involves
once for all everything that will ever happen to him. If we can just get
the numbers down right, we'll see it plainly on the slate. You do me,
and I'll do you." The Accountant hesitated but decided to humor the
man and produced a pencil of remarkable sharpness, as if from thin air.
"Nice trick," said Leibniz. "Now, taking into consideration the elemen-
tary monads, each a world apart and with no possibility of connection
. . . let me see . . . subtract the two, divide by four . . ." The Accoun-
tant did his best to appear thoughtful and to scribble as devotedly as
Leibniz, who continued speaking, "My father died when I was six, you
know. I taught myself from his library and entered the University at
the age of fourteen, but my dissertation was not accepted, and Mother
died shortly after." He peered at the Accountant to see if he was listen-
ing and then returned to his own calculations. "Taking into account
the measure of the limbs and the volume of the flowing white beard,
the Laws of Continuity and Homogeneity, the Identity of Indiscern-

ibles and the Unreality of Matter . . . Hold still, will you? I'm trying to apply the correct . . . My, what big ears you have! Each a universe to itself, I might add. It's a joke," he lied, on misperceiving a wound cross his subject's great brow. "There now," he continued, "Rest assured, I'm making enormous and pristine progress." Again, he misperceived an expression and apologized at once for using the word *enormous*. "The working parts are all really quite diminutive," he added hastily, "as I'm using infinitesimal calculus, which that blowhard Newton believes he devised first. How's yours coming along?" The other made sweeping strokes with the eraser. "I see." It went on like this for the better part of a lifetime. "There, I've just about got it. One last check, and, Yes! Take a look." He spun the slate. A prolonged silence. "Not exactly what you had in mind? The symbols and notations appear arbitrary, I know, but I assure you the calculations are . . ." he trailed off, as the other revealed his work.

"A blank slate?" Leibniz choked. "That's how you made me?"

As if by some miracle then, the infinite arm of that Accountant in the sky plunged through the clouds to stick the slate in the earth.

Leibniz's headstone remained unmarked for another fifty years.

LOCKE

Who proposed that the mind, at birth, is a blank slate and that
all our knowledge comes from experience, which is derived from
sense perception; who perceived the primary qualities of things—
solidity, extension, figure, motion or rest, and number—as insepar-
able from and actually in the body, and the secondary qualities—
colors, sounds, smells, etc.—as existing only in the mind.

So this baby lays this on me: I've got a fresh start, a clean slate here, ex-
cept for all the red I see from sea to sea, but that's just a secondary qual-
ity, right—all in the mind—so it won't matter if I rub it out, and I said,
Pursuing true happiness is the foundation of all liberty, dig, to which
she babbled something about adding that to her constitution before
wondering aloud, in her charming way, if the redskin had any experi-
ence yet of property rights. Not in my experience, said I, which should
make it less-than-difficult for you to lay your claim, though your slate
certainly won't be so clean after that. It's dirty already, she admitted, but
black, too, is a secondary quality, is it not?

I instructed her on tolerance and doubt: Love of truth is not the
same as love of a doctrine proclaimed as truth; God has not been so
sparing to men to make them barely two-legged creatures, leaving it to
Aristotle to make them rational.

If only Locke had learned from his experience that God is as God
does, and whatever selection process He put in place apparently found
rationalizing brains more beneficial than rational ones.

The baby grew to a women and found herself in the chair of Dr. V. S.
Ramachandran, who tricked her brain with simple tapping into ratio-
nalizing that the table before her, whatever its color, was actually part

of her body, such that when he struck it with a hammer, she winced and registered a strong psychogalvanic reflex, something no amount of reasoning could prevent.

And since her experiences were all filtered through God's gift of brain on the way to becoming knowledge, she was doomed, however hopeful her start, to repeat history, discovering along the way that white is also a secondary quality.

So much for a clean slate.

BERKELEY

Who, in wishing to combat the materialism of his time, contended that
even the primary qualities of tables and chairs are only ideas in the
minds of perceivers and cannot exist without being perceived; who him-
self perceived the value of slaves obeying their masters, not as men-
pleasers but as God-fearers, for if a slave falls on the plantation, God is
always there to hear; who attempted to found a seminary for "the children
of savage Americans," acquiring them by theft if necessary before "evil
habits have taken a deep root," that they may be educated in sobriety
of manners and other religious matters and returned as "the ablest and
properest missionaries for spreading the gospel among their countrymen."

Onions, cabbages and other roots and vegetables are in great supply.
There are, however, neither inns, nor carriages, nor bridges over the
rivers, as God has not seen fit to perceive them and thereby make them
perceptible to the savages who fail to see Him. It is our duty, then, to
make visible His grace, and since the savages have already seen us and
would understandably suspect we had designs on their liberty and
property, it would be most expedient to take their children captive, ed-
ucate them in His light and return them as missionaries to their own
countrymen, thus circumventing the natives' great jealousy and preju-
dice towards foreigners and the innovations they introduce.

The shaman couldn't believe his eyes. He tried to dispel the vision
by a shaking of rattles and a shuffling of feet, but the gods held it fixed,
feeding it to him for breakfast, lunch, and dinner. The digesting took
place over several days, during which he sat cross-legged by a fire. At
last, he stood and, stamping his feet, eliminated the evil bile in three
movements before suffocating the flames beneath a blanket, thus re-

ducing their passion to a puff of smoke, which he shepherded toward the rising sun.

The promised funding never arrived for Berkeley's seminary of stolen children, and he returned home eastward across the sea, where God awaited him with carriages and bridges over rivers.

HUME

Whose writings were denounced as works of skepticism and atheism, though
they awakened Kant from his "dogmatic slumbers" and were a central
influence not only on Darwin but on his "bulldog," Huxley; who "castrated"
his chief philosophical work to ingratiate himself with a certain bishop,
deleting his arguments against miracles and other "nobler parts," and still its
publication "fell dead-born from the press"; who failed twice to procure a
professorship, his reputation provoking vocal opposition; whose six volume
History of England, devoted to proving the superiority of Tories to Whigs and
of Scotchmen to Englishmen, finally gave him literary success; who repudiated
the idea of the Self and then wrote his own obituary: "I was a man of mild
dispositions, of command of temper . . . even my love of literary fame,
my ruling passion, never soured my temper, notwithstanding my frequent
disappointment." Unfortunately, he formed a friendship with Rousseau.

When two objects possess the same imagination, the one naturally
induces the other to become more distant to prevent the imagination
from fixing on a conception of "them." The other naturally repels this
strategy, inducing the first to become more distant. In the mind of each
exists the image of a single object. Whether it is the image of itself or
of the other cannot be known, for the image proceeds from imperfec-
tions in its faculties, which are as one with the faculties of the other.
Abstractions immediately crowd in upon us, willing us to perceive the
falsehood of the proposition, though it be true. The mind has produced
an individual idea, yet because the mind belongs not to an individual,
it cannot attach the idea to an individual object, and so the idea is not
really and in fact present to the mind. 'Tis certain the mind would nev-
er have dreamed of distinguishing a figure from the body, but which

body? This is one of the most extraordinary circumstances in the whole affair. To remove this difficulty, we must have recourse to the abundance of abstractions crowding in upon us, the foremost of which being the concrete image of a globe of white marble. The imagination receives only the impression of a white color disposed in a certain form. It cannot distinguish the color from the form and thereby is induced to accept the two objects—color and form—as sharing the same embodiment. Thus, the conception of "body" is expanded to include the two objects possessing the same imagination.

ROUSSEAU

Who rejected reason in favor of the heart and civilization in favor of barbarism; who, Falstaff-like, had a skill for making good sounding arguments off the cuff, and about whom Hume, as if he were describing Lear, said, "He is like a man who was stripped not only of his clothes, but of his skin, and turned out in this situation to combat with the rude and boisterous elements."

F: How now, Jean-Jacques, what time of day is it, lad?

R: What a devil have savages to do with the time of day?

F: O rare! By the Lord, if we're to be savages, I'll be a brave one!

R: What? Play at being savages? Sacrilege.

F: Would that I could play the savage with my hostess of the tavern. Tell me; is she not a most sweet wench?

R: A fair hot wench in flame-colored taffeta. Indeed, you come near me now, Jack.

F: The savage lust, eh? The savage appetite, the beast on the prowl? Governed, as the sea is, by our noble mistress the moon—

R: Governed by the heart.

F: —under whose countenance we steal.

R: Tis no sin for a man to do what comes naturally to him.

F: Indeed, no, sweet rogue . . . 'tis a crime of the passions.

R: What barbarous iteration!

F: Is this not a play we're acting?

R: Savages don't act plays. Plato disapproves of them, and the Catholic Church refuses to marry or bury actors.

F: Yet, how many savages they've sent to their graves.

R: Prithee, trouble me no more with the vanity of thy reason. Take note. Herein, I grime my face with filth, blanket my loins, and with presented nakedness outface the persecutions of thy hot winds.

F: Whoever smelt it dealt it.

R: Is there no virtue extant? By breaking through the foul and ugly mists of vapors that seem to suffocate, I will imitate the sun and be more wondered at.

F: More wondered at indeed. What hadst thou to eat, lad? A cold capon's leg? Thou hast done much harm upon me and art indeed able to corrupt a saint. God forgive thee for it!

R: I care not. I'll so offend, to make offence a skill. Blow, winds, and crack my cheeks!

F: O! O! 'tis foul!

R: Singe his white head! And thou, all-shaking thunder, strike flat his thick rotundity!

F: Villain! Dog! What a plague hast thou set upon us.

R: The fruits of this earth belong to us all.

F: Keep thy fruits to thyself! Have you no culture? Thou hast taken the basest shape that ever poverty, in contempt of man, brought near to beast. What need you of this transformation?

R: Reason not the need. When nature calls, a man must answer with all his heart.

F: If that was your heart, I'm a gib cat. You see too much of what is not there, mad wag, and not enough of what is. Break through these contagious clouds. I see in thee still the chance of a good amendment of life.

R: Alas, that's past praying for. I should have been that I am, had the maidenliest star in the firmament twinkled on my breeding.

F: It stands to reason.

R: A pox on reason! Thou art fat-witted with drinking of old sack!

F: And thou art as thin-witted with scavenging as the snickering hyena.

R: [Pause] Alas, my most durable happiness was but a dream. The vapors dissipated and with them that noble rascal Sir John, with whom I could have jousted to the end of time.

KANT

Who sought to resolve disputes between empirical and rationalist approaches, arguing that experiential knowledge, unprocessed by reason, is purely subjective, while knowledge from reason alone, as in Plato's world of ideas, is theoretical illusion; who, having experienced wind, wrote a treatise on it; who, though he never in his life traveled more than ten miles from Königsberg, Prussia, was greatly effected by the earthquake of Lisbon, one of the deadliest in history (and used by Rousseau to argue for a more naturalistic way of life away from cities); who gathered all the news pamphlets he could on the subject and published three separate texts on it, being one of the first in history to propose natural rather than supernatural causes: the shifting of subterranean caverns full of hot gases, an idea that ultimately proved incorrect.

Hot, sulfurous wind. Not an experience for the faint of heart. Yet, one must stick one's nose in it, so to speak, to formulate any theories on the matter. One can easily measure the dimensions of the crack; touch the slightly protruding, creased, and somewhat dry vent hole; hear the rumblings within and feel the hot blast against the face; sniff out the chemical components and measure the pressure, temperature and volume of the gas, but only with the application of reason can one then draw conclusions from the sensorial experience, conclusions as to what purpose harvested the elements towards such a noxious end, what force propelled the gas thus and from what deep caverns it must have emanated.

Of course, the wind was merely the product of elephantine digestion, but how can a man know this when neither his faulty senses nor his limited reason, nor any combination thereof can conceive the whole, diseased elephant?

DARWIN

Whose original idea was not the doctrine of evolution (the different forms of life had developed gradually from a common ancestry), something already maintained by his grandfather and others, but the motive force behind it.

My work is now nearly finished. It is, therefore, of the highest importance to breed. Sterility has been said to be the bane of our culture. My reproductive system, however, has not been affected. Still, peculiarities appearing in the males of our domestic breed suggest cattle could appear in the offspring. It is a risk I must take. Seedlings from the same fruit yielding deaf cats with blue eyes, horses with goat udders, ducks so unlike those found in the wild. The whole enterprise has been carried to an absurd extreme, and so, after much deliberation, I have chosen to take up domestic relations with pigeons, which utter a very different coo from the other breeds, not to mention their tail feathers being carried so erect that in good birds the head and tail touch. Since the oil gland is quite aborted, I will have to supply my own lubricant and do not believe any ornithologist would chide me for doing so. Great as the differences are between the breeds, great also are the likenesses. These birds, for example, bear a striking resemblance to my mother. I have never met a pigeon fancier, who was not fully convinced of the same. Breeding freely with them requires as much. It is certain that several of our eminent breeders have, even within a single lifetime, modified to a large extent some breeds of cattle and sheep.

Let us then consider the prodding force behind it.

HEGEL

Who held that the world is not a collection of hard units, such as tables, fruit bowls and people, but is rather all of one whole, which he called the Absolute and found more akin to a complex organism than to the simple substance adhered to by Parmenides and Spinoza; who believed each successive appearance of the mind to itself dissolves into a more comprehensive and integrated form and that the nature of reality can be deduced from the sole consideration that it must not contradict itself.

Do I contradict myself?
Very well then I contradict myself,
(I am large, I contain multitudes.)

Not a quarter-century after Hegel's death, he rose and took flight, full in the breast of the as-yet beardless American.

Speeding through space, speeding through heaven and the stars,
Speeding amid the seven satellites and the broad ring, and the
diameter of eighty thousand miles,
Speeding with tail'd meteors, throwing fire-balls like the rest . . .

. . . moving forward then and now and forever,
Gathering and showing more always and with velocity,
Infinite

To be in any form, what is that?
(Round and round we go . . . and ever come back thither) . . .

What appeared then to Hegel from such a vantage of multiple forms?

Where the quail is whistling betwixt the woods and the wheatlot,
Where the bat flies in the Seventh-month eve, where the great gold-
    bug drops through the dark,
Where the brook puts out of the roots of the old tree and flows to the
    meadow,
Where cattle stand and shake away flies with the tremulous shudder-
    ing of their hides . . .

Where trip-hammers crash, where the press is whirling its cylinders,
Where the human heart beats with terrible throes under its ribs,
Where the pear-shaped balloon is floating aloft . . .

Hegel's own heart was the pear-shaped balloon, ever rising through
the vapors and ever expanding from the vapors within, until Whitman
burst out, for

All truths wait in all things,
They neither hasten their own delivery nor resist it,
They do not need the obstetric forceps of the surgeon . . .

The curling string and filmy tatters of rubber drifted earthward once
more, alighting on a dirty Manhattan boulevard, where they were
trampled over and kicked by a multitude of separate bodies in a land of
rugged individualism.

Yet some sense could be made of how this thumbnail consciousness
successively appeared to itself as it disintegrated into greater and great-
er integration with the whole.

Years later, the last traces of rubber and string were spied and eventually sung about by a bearded bard who chanced to pass in a carriage, while muttering to the driver,

The damp of the night drives deeper into my soul.

BYRON

Whose grandfather, Vice Admiral "Foulweather Jack," circumnavigated the globe; whose father, Captain "Mad Jack," married his mother for her fortune but squandered it; whose first recollections were of his parent's fierce quarrels; who feared his mother's despotism and, worse, that he'd inherited her vulgarity; who mocked her for being short and fat, as she mocked him for being lame; whose nurse combined wickedness with the strictest Calvinist theology; who himself combined the two; who, when his great-uncle, "the Wicked Lord," died, became the 6th Baron Bryon of Rochdale at age ten; who believed wickedness was a hereditary curse, and, since he must be remarkable, he would be remarkable as a sinner; who felt himself an equal of the greatest sinners; who, to Alfred de Musset, was an accomplice in the wicked work of instilling the poison of melancholy into the cheerful Gallic soul.

Hi. My name is George. My bad guy name is Baby Face, 'causa my curly hair and chubby cheeks, my tender skin and pink lips, which, no matter how I tickle 'em, lie there fat and lame, like a pair of dead Penis fish in a bowl.

She walks in beauty, like the night

If you believe that, I've got some land on the Greek Isles, but I made a woman out of her just the same, gave her the ol' club foot, if you know what I mean, though she was the house maid and three times my pre-pubescent age. Or was that my half sister, Augusta, after I'd begged her to consider me as more than a brother. Ah, well, pleasure's a sin, and sin's a pleasure.

"Trust Byron." That's on my coat of arms, along with a sultry mermaid on top of some horses. Or is it the other way around? It always was in my imagination, I suppose—"Trust Byron," echoing over the she-devil's animal groans of "Pain's a pleasure," and sometimes, "Pleasure's a pain."

I have not loved the world, nor the world me;

Thank the Lord my great-uncle saw fit to keel over and make me Lord. Not God, mind you. Let Nietzsche make himself God's equal. This Lord is Satan's.

What I have done is done; I bear within
A torture which could nothing gain from thine[.]

And you? What are you in here for?

SCHOPENHAUER

Who appealed more to artists and writers than to professional
philosophers; who loathed the hypocrisy he found at boarding school,
and even more the prospect of following his father into a business
career; who longed for an academic life, which was ultimately made
possible by his father's death, most likely by suicide; who considered
will as ethically evil, and our world to be driven by a continually
dissatisfied will, continually seeking satisfaction.

So, Will and I were in a bar, and Will says to me, "Whoever has learnt
logic for practical purposes is like him who would teach a beaver to
make its own dam."

"You sound dissatisfied," I told him, refilling his glass.

"If I am condemned to roam this Earth as a clump of busybody mol-
ecules driven by desire to mince and mix up what is put into them,
then I shall costume myself hereafter as the beaver, suck my nourish-
ment from a twig, and refuse to be taught anything until that day comes
when I can shit phantasies so concrete as to be impenetrable by man
or machine."

Perhaps a little background is needed. I had been expounding on
the thought that we are nothing but organic machines, mixing up what
is put into them and converting the nutrients into phantasies, castles
in the air, while excreting the more concrete matter as waste. "By logic
and reason," I said to him, "man has attempted to reverse this process
so that his castles could be made of the more concrete matter, but so far
his resources have proved insufficient to the task."

"I shall endeavor then," said Will, "to make my own dam, a shel-
ter from both the direct light of the sun and the borrowed light of the

moon. It is there I'll make my daily bread, though the result be some-what soggy." And, as if to illustrate the point, he dipped a hunk of bread in beer and proceeded to wipe his ass with it.

"Continually seeking some sort of satisfaction, eh? Will that just about do it then? No, of course not. Nothing ever has been enough, and nothing ever will be enough, though you fool yourself that *enough* is just around the corner. You're a slave, Will, a slave to your will, an organic machine condemned to walk this Earth, and so I say to you, seek refuge instead in a beaver's dam is a beaver's dam is a beaver's dam . . . until you dynamite the dam."

"Ah," countered Will, "but that would require an effort of will, and I for one . . ."

I took his tired ass home and put us to bed.

NIETZSCHE

Who called ordinary human beings the "bungled and botched" and saw
no objection to their suffering if it was necessary for the production of
even one great man; who thought it compulsory for higher men to make
war upon the masses, seeing in all directions the mediocre joining hands
to make themselves masters; whose "noble" man is ruthless, cunning,
cruel, and concerned only with his own power; who found women con-
temptible creatures with only dancing and nonsense in their minds.

That blockhead, John Stuart Mill! What is right for one man is *not* right
for another, especially in the case when both men are one. I may recline
in an office chair and don the professor's mild sport coat, but just let me
get to that mythical phone booth and, like a tiger, tear these vestments
from my chest. I will do such things—what they are yet I know not, but
they won't be wasted on the bungled and the botched. Ode to a Grecian
Urn is worth any number of old ladies, as women are cats anyway, or
birds, or cows at best, and Lois Lane's frivolous and deceitful snatch
shall never get near enough to snatch my whip. I'm on to her games
and choose to keep my distance. Damn Rousseau for making women
seem interesting! Damn Socrates for corrupting the noble Athenian
youth! Damn Plato for his damnable moral instruction! Damn Kant!
Damn Mill! Damn Buddha and Christ! The terror of the earth shall
rain down! You think I have no Will to Power, that my courage is lim-
ited to scribbling manifestos in seclusion? The pen is mightier than
the sword, my friend, and this sword shall cut through huge swaths of
men, for one ought to desire the slaughter of our whole civilization if
such a reward as one great man be the result. Democracy? Fie! Rule by
the botched? None of whom, I might add, wear mustaches so noble as
mine. (He combed his fingers through the bushy caterpillar above his

lip, rose, and ever-so-gently placed the stylus on the wax-coated cylinder. Wagner's *Ring*.) Ah, that's better. Music to sooth the savage soul. Did I say *sooth*? I meant *stir*. Now, where was I? The Will to Power? Death to God and ordinary men? Damn repentance and redemption! We are heirs to the conscience-vivisection and self-crucifixion of two thousand years. Christianity tames the heart, breaks the spirit, exploits moments of debility to convert assurance to anxiety; it poisons the noblest instincts, infects them with disease, until their strength turns inward, against themselves—until the strong perish through excessive self-contempt. (He sniffed at the fat caterpillar.) Hmmm. (He sniffed twice more.) Sour cow's milk . . . If only it were the sweet, warm milk of mother's breast. Did I say that out loud?

So ran The Secret Life of Friedrich Nietzsche.

MARX

Whose family converted to Christianity so that his father could pursue his
career as a lawyer in the face of Prussia's anti-Jewish laws; who studied
law in Bonn and Berlin, where he became interested in the philosophical
ideas of the Young Hegelians and compared the views of Democritus
and Epicurus in his PhD thesis; who turned to economics and politics and
became one of the biggest influences in the creation of the modern world;
whose works, including Horse Feathers, Animals Crackers, and Duck Soup,
are often confused with those of an American family comedy act.

INTERVIEWER: You were born into the upper middle class.

MARX: I sent the club a wire, stating, PLEASE ACCEPT MY
RESIGNATION. I DON'T WANT TO BELONG TO
ANY CLUB THAT WILL ACCEPT ME AS A MEMBER.

I: You were a precocious schoolchild.

M: Outside of a dog, a book is man's best friend. Inside of a dog, it's
too dark to read.

I: You took part in both the French and the German revolutions.

M: I danced before Napoleon. No, Napoleon danced before me—
in fact, he danced a hundred years before me.

I: You opposed the romantics.

M: I came here for a party and what do I get? Nothing. Not even Ice
cream. Therefore, if any form of pleasure is exhibited, report
to me and it will be prohibited.

I: Let me try another approach. The driving force, for you, is really man's relation to matter, is it not, of which the most important part is his mode of production?

M: Just for that I'm not going to give you the job I was going to give you. I'm writing a screenplay, you know, in which the workers of the world unite.

I: What's it called?

M: Workers of the World Unite.

I: I see. I'll try again. You say both subject and object, both the knower and the thing known, are in a continual process of mutual adaptation, which you call "dialectical" because it is never fully completed.

M: Not in your case anyway.

I: Very well then. After the failure of the revolution, you retreated here to London, troubled by poverty, illness, and the deaths of children.

M: Why don't you bore a hole in yourself and let the sap run out.

I: Are you a man or a mouse?

M: Put a piece of cheese on the floor and you'll find out.

I: Oh, you are too much wrapped up in the problems of your time.

M: Those are my principles, and if you don't like them . . . well, I have others.

I: I'm afraid our time is up.

M: Time flies like an arrow. Fruit flies like a banana.

I: Thank you for such an . . . illustrative evening.

M: I've had a perfectly wonderful evening, but this wasn't it.

BERGSON

Who opposed the reduction of spirit to matter, arguing against Ribot's claims that brain science had proved memory was of a material nature, and against Descartes's dualism for separating in space rather than time; who believed spirit housed the past and memory was its mortar.

Bergson? Wherefore art thou Bergson? Behold Mama and Papa Bergson. Behold Proust, your best man, and James, your great friend. Behold the Nobel committee. Yet, who or what exactly does memory behold? I am haunted by this notion: I shall be remembered as a thing. Cleaved off by reason, as the butcher cleaves the body whole into body parts and slaps labels on the packages. *You* think; therefore, I am not.

Did I produce circular arguments in my time? Very well, then, I produced them, but I produced them with unbridled intuition, the stuff of spirit, not reason.

What will it be then in your undiscovered country? Blake's fourfold vision or Newton's sleep? If I'm to check my memory at the door, I very much doubt the former, for perception without memory, even perception of your country, is mere matter.

A man falls into a well, a well of his making. In it grow the flowers of the past: his birth in Paris to Jewish parents, his childhood in London, his loss of faith in adolescence, his early education in mathematics and solving of a problem posed by Pascal, his shift to philosophy and subsequent years of teaching, his marriage to Proust's cousin and the birth of their deaf daughter, his brother-in-law's founding of the Hermetic Order of the Golden Dawn, his investigation into perception and memory and the problems of the relation of spirit and body, his observations of hypnosis sessions and interest in the role of unconscious memories, his election as president of the London based Society for Psychical Research, his little piggies that went to market, his little piggies that stayed home, his little piggies that had roast beef, his little piggies that had none, his little piggies that went *wee wee wee* . . . his refusal of exemptions from anti-Semitic regulations, his contracting of the cold that killed him, or so it was rumored, while waiting in line to register as a Jew.

Show thyself, why don't you! Are you a poet or a butcher?

Here I sit, as if at the bottom of a well, in some prolonged purgatory, not even knowing if this is all there ever was.

DEWEY

Who criticized the rote learning of facts in schools, arguing that truth
is not static and final, as tradition holds, but biological and evolutionary;
who proposed that children should be taught weaving, carpentry, cook-
ing, and gardening since knowledge arises from an active adaptation
of the human organism to its environment.

Believe me, if I were to do just as I feel, I should sit down or stand up
and not spend so much time here (he pointed to his head). More of
my waking life than I should care to admit was whiled away in this
cauliflower. Still, civilized activity is too complex to be carried on with-
out smoothed roads. It requires signals and junction points. A savage
mind may travel well in a jungle, but—what was that? Did you hear it?
A scrawl on a sketchpad? I must confess; I am distracted with the fear
of being drawn by a native of this place. I take a position and straight
away one appears from out of the brambles, wielding a turkey feather
and a simple parchment. Only once have I been afforded the pleasure
of seeing the finished product. My ears were drawn as bookends to a
jungle of squawking parrots, lying lizards, and shrieking chimpanzees.
Below it, the caption read: "The problem of attaining correct habits of
reflection would be much easier than it is, did not the different modes
of thinking blend insensibly into one another." I recovered my speech
only just in time to berate the barbarian before he blended back into the
scenery: "You might have benefitted from a more manual education!"
What do they teach them in the jungle these days? All philosophy and
no dexterity. I should draw a better parrot were I the parrot itself.

And you! Where do you think you're going?

Ah, but you remained right where you were, beside the only gravestone on the University of Vermont campus. It was Dewey who went, breathed back beneath the stone, where the mutual adjustment between organism and environment was proving difficult at best.

EINSTEIN

Whose theories gave victories to Leibniz over Newton and to Heraclitus over Parmenides; who, on the eve of World War II, endorsed a letter to President Roosevelt, alerting him to the potential development of "extremely powerful bombs of a new type" and recommending that the U.S. begin similar research; who, with Bertrand Russell, signed the Russell–Einstein Manifesto, which highlighted the danger of nuclear weapons.

A practically rigid body lies in a practically straight line, hovering over Times Square. A pedestrian who observes the misdeed from a footpath remains ignorant of how the body alters its position with time. Imagine two clocks. The one held by the pedestrian is broken, while the one strapped to the body moves in a step-motherly fashion. It is not difficult to understand why. The body must alter its position with time. It appears inevitable that I should repeat myself. Matters of elegance ought to be left to the tailor and the cobbler, each of whom works busily now at his craft in case the body should come down and need clothing and footwear. As is well known, a body removed sufficiently far from another body continues in a state of rest. Thus, from the point of view of the body over Times Square, the cobbler remains at rest, and the footwear will never be finished. No wonder the body doesn't come down. We now proceed to the name. A name has been assigned. It is not difficult to understand why. A name corresponds more or less to an object in nature—in this case, the body, however unnatural the pedestrian may consider it. Even a practically rigid body deserves a name. That is, until it is completely rigid, and we call it a corpse, at which time everyone begins the process of forgetting its name, a process that takes time. Imagine two clocks. If the clock on the corpse has stopped, its name will not be forgotten.

MATERIALS USED

Aristophanes, *Birds*; *Clouds*.
Bertrand Russell, *A History of Western Philosophy*.
Walt Whitman, "Song of Myself," *Leaves of Grass*.
William Shakespeare, *Henry IV*, Part I; *King Lear*.

Pythagoras:

> http://www-groups.dcs.st-and.ac.uk/~history/Biographies/Pythagoras
> .html

Heraclitus:

> The fragments of the work of Heraclitus of Ephesus on Nature
> http://en.wikipedia.org/wiki/Four_temperaments
> http://en.wikipedia.org/wiki/Heraclitus
> http://en.wikipedia.org/wiki/Humorism

Empedocles:

> http://plato.stanford.edu/entries/empedocles/

Anaxagoras:

> http://www-history.mcs.st-and.ac.uk/Biographies/Anaxagoras.html
> http://www.egs.edu/library/anaxagoras
> http://history.hanover.edu/texts/presoc/anaxagor.html#frag1
> http://en.wikipedia.org/wiki/Anaxagoras

Protagoras:

> http://www.ancient.eu.com/protagoras/
> http://en.wikipedia.org/wiki/Protagoras
> http://en.wikipedia.org/wiki/Protagoras_(dialogue)

Socrates:

> http://plato.stanford.edu/entries/socrates/

Plato:

> *The Republic*

Aristotle:

Poetics

http://www.biography.com/people/aristotle-9188415

Plotinus:

http://plato.stanford.edu/entries/plotinus/

http://en.wikipedia.org/wiki/Plotinus

Augustine:

Confessions

http://en.wikipedia.org/wiki/Augustine_of_Hippo

Benedict:

http://www.ccel.org/ccel/benedict

http://en.wikipedia.org/wiki/Benedict_of_Nursia

Gregory the Great:

http://en.wikipedia.org/wiki/Pope_Gregory_I

John the Scot:

The Division of Nature (http://www.users.globalnet.co.uk/~alfar2/cosmos
/Eriugena.pdf)

http://en.wikipedia.org/wiki/Johannes_Scotus_Eriugena

Aquinas:

http://plato.stanford.edu/entries/aquinas/

http://dhspriory.org/thomas/ContraGentiles1.htm#1

http://en.wikipedia.org/wiki/Thomas_Aquinas

Machiavelli:

http://plato.stanford.edu/entries/machiavelli/

Erasmus:

The Praise of Folly (trans. by John Wilson)

http://en.wikisource.org/wiki/The_Praise_of_Folly

http://en.wikipedia.org/wiki/Desiderius_Erasmus

http://en.wikipedia.org/wiki/Desiderius_Erasmus#Education_and
   _scholarship
More:
   http://en.wikipedia.org/wiki/Thomas_More
Copernicus:
   http://plato.stanford.edu/entries/copernicus/
   http://www.webexhibits.org/calendars/year-text-Copernicus.html
   http://en.wikipedia.org/wiki/Nicolaus_Copernicus
   http://en.wikipedia.org/wiki/De_revolutionibus_orbium_coelestium
Kepler:
   On Firmer Fundaments of Astrology (trans. Marie Čamachová, cor-
      rected by Hana Neumannová)
   The Harmonies of the World (trans. Charles Glenn Wallis)
   http://plato.stanford.edu/entries/kepler/
   http://plato.stanford.edu/entries/kepler/#OptMetLig
   http://en.wikipedia.org/wiki/Johannes_Kepler
   http://en.wikipedia.org/wiki/Platonic_solid
Newton:
   Principia Mathematica
   http://en.wikipedia.org/wiki/Isaac_Newton#Personal_life
Bacon:
   http://www.westegg.com/bacon/atheism.html
   http://en.wikipedia.org/wiki/Francis_Bacon
Hobbes:
   https://scholarsbank.uoregon.edu/xmlui/bitstream/handle/1794
      /748/leviathan.pdf
   http://en.wikipedia.org/wiki/Accident_(philosophy)

Descartes:

Meditations of First Philosophy

http://plato.stanford.edu/entries/descartes/

http://en.wikipedia.org/wiki/Ren%C3%A9_Descartes

Spinoza:

http://plato.stanford.edu/entries/spinoza/

http://en.wikipedia.org/wiki/Baruch_Spinoza

Leibniz:

http://www.egs.edu/library/gottfried-wilhelm-leibniz/biography/

http://en.wikipedia.org/wiki/Gottfried_Wilhelm_Leibniz

Locke:

http://plato.stanford.edu/entries/locke/]:

http://en.wikipedia.org/wiki/John_Locke

http://en.wikipedia.org/wiki/An_Essay_Concerning_Human_
Understanding

Berkeley:

*A Proposal for the Better Supplying of Churches in Our Foreign Plan-
tations, and for Converting the Savage Americans to Christianity*

http://www-history.mcs.st-and.ac.uk/Biographies/Berkeley.html

http://en.wikipedia.org/wiki/George_Berkeley

Hume:

A Treatise of Human Nature

http://plato.stanford.edu/entries/hume/

Rousseau:

Confessions (http://www2.hn.psu.edu/faculty/jmanis/rousseau/confessions
.pdf)

Discourse on Inequality

Social Contract (http://mongolianmind.com/wp-content/uploads/2012
/11/Rousseau_contrat-social-1221.pdf)

http://en.wikipedia.org/wiki/Jean-Jacques_Rousseau

Kant:

http://plato.stanford.edu/entries/kant/

http://en.wikipedia.org/wiki/Immanuel_Kant

http://en.wikipedia.org/wiki/1755_Lisbon_earthquake

http://en.wikipedia.org/wiki/Noumenon

Darwin:

On the Origin of Species

Hegel:

http://plato.stanford.edu/entries/hegel/

http://en.wikipedia.org/wiki/The_Phenomenology_of_Spirit

Byron:

http://www.poetryfoundation.org/bio/lord-byron

http://en.wikipedia.org/wiki/Lord_Byron

Schopenhauer:

The World as Will and Representation

Marx:

Das Kapital

http://plato.stanford.edu/entries/marx/

http://www.marx-brothers.org/info/quotes.htm

http://en.wikipedia.org/wiki/Karl_Marx

Bergson:

http://plato.stanford.edu/entries/bergson/

http://en.wikipedia.org/wiki/Henri_Bergson

http://en.wikipedia.org/wiki/Matter_and_Memory

Dewey:

China, Japan, and the U.S.A.: Present-Day Conditions in the Far East and Their Bearing on the Washington Conference

Letters from China and Japan

How We Think

Human Nature and Conduct: An Introduction to Social Psychology

http://deweycenter.siu.edu/pdf/Dewey_Bio.pdf

http://www.iep.utm.edu/dewey/]

http://www.spartacus.schoolnet.co.uk/USAdewey.htm

http://www.biography.com/people/john-dewey-9273497#awesm
    =~oDqGJOsCQJlhx2

http://en.wikipedia.org/wiki/John_Dewey#cite_note-48

Einstein:

Relativity: The Special and General Theory

http://en.wikipedia.org/wiki/Albert_Einstein

ACKNOWLEDGMENTS

Thanks to the editors and staffs of the following journals where these poems first appeared (some in different versions):

Brooklyn Rail: "Aquinas," "Empedocles," "Erasmus," "Intro-
duction," "Socrates" (grouped as "Russell" and nominated for
a Pushcart Prize); *Denver Quarterly*: "Anaxagoras," "Hobbes,"
"Hume," "Leibniz"; *Doctor T. J. Eckleburg Review*: "Plato" (finalist
for The Franz Kafka Award in Fiction, 2014); *Web Conjunctions*:
"Bacon," "Benedict," "Gregory the Great," "More," "Plotinus."